Mou...
Pyr...

The Pyrenees, extending ... France from Spain, and ... dramatically beautiful ... because the flowers of ... Europe and the Mediterranean region.

This book will help identify many of the lovely flowers that inhabit the meadows, forests and high alpine regions of these mountains and is designed particularly for those with little knowledge of plant families. It is not a botanical guide but it is hoped that those who have such knowledge will also find it useful, interesting and enjoyable.

In association with Collett's Mountain Holidays
www.colletts.co.uk

Introduction

The Pyrenees extend over 270 miles from Atlantic to Mediterranean, separating France and Spain and enveloping tiny Andorra, while the Picos de Europa is the most prominent range in the chain of mountains that extends along the north coast of Spain. They have much in common. They are both scenically dramatic, beautiful and botanically fascinating because they sit where the flowers of Northern Europe meet those of Southern Europe and the Mediterranean.

Each range has a moister, greener northern side and a drier, less verdant southern face. They have high peaks, ridges and glacial cirques, most often of limestone but with areas of acid rocks and contrasting flora. Many species can be found in both ranges but they also have lovely and interesting endemics.

The high pastures are grazed by cattle, sheep and horses which, following the traditions of many centuries, are driven on foot from lower ground in Spring amid much celebration, returning in Autumn. These high places are readily accessible, in the Pyrenees by high passes crossing the international border and in the Picos by a superb cable car at Fuente De.

Sheltered valleys, and in the Picos three deep limestone gorges, harbour a wealth of more tender species. Olive trees, and Mediterranean bulbs and orchids flourish, while high above, only a short distance away as the eagles and vultures fly, are wild mountain tops where the loveliest of alpine flowers grow in the bleakest of climatic conditions.

How to use this book

Limitations of space in this small volume mean that only the most beautiful, frequently encountered and interesting species have been chosen to give a representative, but by no means complete, introduction to the species of each mountain range.

To help those unfamiliar with plant families species are arranged by:
1. flower colour, then
2. the habitat in which they are principally found and finally
3. alphabetical order of their Latin names.

Note that:

- many species grow in a variety of habitats, at very different altitudes and may display a variety of colours.

- those requiring specialised conditions (e.g. scree or rock crevice) usually found at a particular altitude may thrive higher or lower if the conditions are right.

- the height of a plant may be governed by altitude, location and biological variation. Flowering dates also depend on altitude, aspect and weather.

Botanical and technical language has been kept to a minimum. See the Glossary on page 5 which illustrates botanical terms that are used.

For the reasons above, detailed data on dimensions, altitude range and plant structure are rarely given. Features obvious from the photographs are not always described. Please study the images with care. They illustrate key features that aid identification and show the great beauty of the flowers and the mountain habitats in which they live.

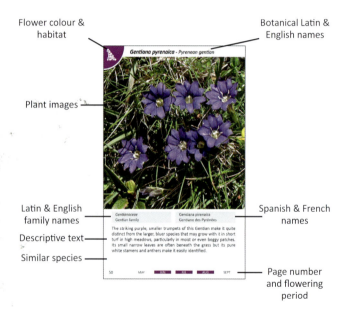

Flower colour & habitat

Botanical Latin & English names

Plant images

Latin & English family names

Descriptive text

Similar species

Spanish & French names

Page number and flowering period

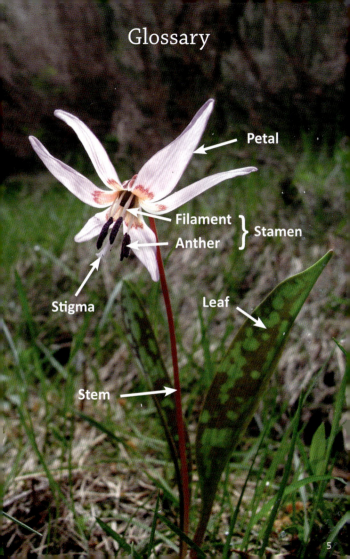

Valley Meadows

 Traditional hay or grazing meadows at altitudes below the tree line can be so rich in flowering species and so appealing to the eye, that it is easy to forget that they are man-made and not wild or natural. If not regularly grazed or cut shrub and tree seedlings would encroach and they would eventually revert to woodland.

Likewise, rich flower meadows can be rapidly reduced in diversity by the application of fertiliser, promoting the growth of grasses and suppressing flowering species that cannot tolerate high levels of nitrogen.

The best meadows are those that have thrived with little enrichment for generations. Annual, biennial and perennial flowering species, orchids and bulbous plants continually regenerate from seed to create a magnificent kaleidoscope of colours in spring and summer, often followed by a smaller selection of dwarf bulbs that flower in autumn.

Woodland

In the Pyrenees and Picos trees often grow to a higher altitude than in the mountains of northern Europe. There are coniferous species on high but the greater glory is the magnificent deciduous forests below of birch, beech, sweet chestnut and oak, both deciduous and evergreen. Many ancient and splendid specimens can be found.

Areas of dappled shade, before the trees come into leaf, provide perfect conditions for spring flowering species. In woodland glades flutter colourful butterflies while mosses, fungi and lichens thrive in damp shady areas, forming a very different ecosystem to the wild open mountains above.

Note how adaptable many species are to contrasting habitats. You may find high snowmelt species like Narcissi flowering in the light shade of open woodland. Conversely Erythroniums and even Hepaticas grow in sheltered spots in the high mountains, perhaps survivors of a time when the climate permitted a shrub layer to grow there.

High Mountain Meadows

Above the tree line in the high mountains extend pastures, sometimes grazed in summer and under deep snow in winter. Here live a superbly adapted community of flowering plants that rest until snowmelt and then burst into beautiful bloom. In the short mountain summer they must attract a pollinator, set seed and prepare for their next long dormancy.

Thin soils on well-drained rocky substrates provide the conditions required by such species. Minerals carried in the melt water and the intense mountain sunlight give the nutrients required to create wonderful natural rock gardens of lovely flowers. The rugged mountain terrain is carpeted with stunning Gentians, Pulsatillas and Saxifragas and exquisite dwarf Narcissi and Fritillarias.

Other species thrive in wet, boggy areas or by mountain streams – look for high mountain buttercup species, Primulas and carnivorous Pinguiculas.

Rocks, Peaks & Scree

 It is a curious but wonderful paradox that perhaps the most beautiful flowering plants grow in the most inhospitable places. In tight rock crevices, on cliffs and in loose rocky screes, exposed to the harsh mountain climate, are found exquisite jewel-like species that thrive where more robust plants could not exist.

Usually very low-growing and mat-forming, these species have long root systems delving deep into the rocks. This secures them against fierce winds and rock movements and enables them to find beneath the surface the modest nutrients and moisture they require. Their leaves are often succulent or covered in hairs to help preserve moisture. They may form tight cushions of small rosettes, each bearing a beautiful flower that may completely cloak the foliage – a glorious spectacle and highlight of any visit to the high mountains.

The Pyrenees

Picos de Europa

Aquilegia pyrenaica - Pyrenean columbine

Ranunculaceae
Buttercup family

Aquileña del Pirineo
Ancolie des Pyrénées

Bright blue flowers rise on the divided stems of this elegant species, only found in the Pyrenees and Northern Spain. Lift the flower head to examine the beautiful, symmetrical interior and note the long, straight spurs of the petals, the ends curved like the talons of an eagle, from which its name derives. Aquilegia vulgaris (inset) is a larger species with round, not straight, spurs.

MAY   JUN   JUL   AUG   SEPT

Brimeura amethystina - Pyrenean hyacinth

Hyacinthaceae
Hyacinth family

Jacinto pirenaico
Jacinthe améthyste

A common, pretty, small bulb of rocky dry places, roadsides and scrub. Above long grass-like leaves rise stems on one side of which hang delicate bell-shaped light blue flowers.

See Scilla lilio-hyacinthus p33

MAY   JUN   JUL   AUG   SEPT

Campanula patula - *Spreading bellflower*

Campanulaceae
Bellflower family

Campanillas
Campanule étalée

On slender stems, in meadows, grassy places and on roadsides, this species has spreading clusters of upward-facing large but delicate pale blue flowers with prominent white anthers. Usually quite tall but diminutive forms can be found (inset).

Carduncellus mitissimus - *Carduncellus*

Asteraceae
Daisy family

Cardo sin espinas
Cardoncelle

A spineless relative of the thistles (mitissmus means 'very soft') that forms loose mats on wasteland and meadow edges with prostrate branches carrying finely cut blue-green leaves. The flowers, equally prostrate, are pale blue with dark blue stamens tipped with powdery white.

MAY   JUN   JUL   AUG   SEPT

Echium vulgare - Viper's bugloss

Boraginaceae	Viborera
Borage family	Vipérine commune

Very common in rocky places, screes and meadows at all altitudes on well-drained limestone. Erect hairy stems carry spikes of vivid blue flowers opening from pink buds. Occasional pink and white forms are found. The stamens protrude from the flowers a little like a snake's tongue.

MAY　JUN　JUL　AUG　SEPT

Eryngium bourgatii - Pyrenean sea-holly

Umbelliferae
Carrot family

Cardo de Puerto
Chardon bleu des Pyrénées

A very common plant at all altitudes from lower meadows to the highest rocky places. It has unmistakable prickly leaves marked with silver and stems streaked with blue. Flowers form a tight cluster surrounded by spiny bracts, all coloured icy blue.

Jasione laevis - *Sheep's bit*

| Campanulaceae | Botón azul |
| Bellflower family | Jasione vivace |

The Spanish name 'blue button' perfectly describes this species, which rambles gently through grassy meadows on limestone. Eye-catching clusters of tiny blue flowers with narrow pointed petals and white stamens. Could be confused with a Globularia but the flower structure is quite different.

See Globularia nudicaulis p42, Globularia repens p41

MAY · JUN · JUL · AUG · SEPT

Linum narbonense - Beautiful flax

Linaceae
Flax family

Lino azul
Lin de Narbonne

Showy and vibrant plant of dry rocky places, wasteland and roadsides with spectacular azure-blue flowers on greyish-green stems with long pointed leaves. Not found in Northern Europe but extends through the Mediterranean to North Africa.

See Linum viscosum p66

MAY JUN JUL AUG SEPT

Polygala alpestris - *Alpine milkwort*

Polygalaceae	Lechera
Milkwort family	Polygale alpestre

Very common family of similar species in grassy meadows and roadsides on limestone. Spreading stems creep through taller surrounding vegetation and produce clusters of bright blue flowers with contrasting white stamens. This species has a cluster of upward-pointing leaves below the flowers.

See Polygala comosa p74

Scilla verna - Spring squill

Asparagaceae	Escilla de primavera
Asparagus family	Scille de printemps

The upward-facing pale blue flowers of this dwarf bulb cover the early spring meadows, rising above the short grass in dense clusters above vertical fleshy green leaves. The anthers are an attractively contrasting dark blue.

See Scilla lilio-hyacinthus p33

Veronica ponae - Spiked Pyrenean speedwell

Scrophulariaceae
Figwort family

Veronica de Gouan
Véronique de Gouan

Unlike many Veronicas this species has upright flower spikes with clusters of large, delicate-blue flowers with white centres and anthers. Pointed, toothed leaves and woody stems. Grows only in the Pyrenees and Northern Spain in moist rocky areas, usually in shade.

MAY | **JUN** | **JUL** | **AUG** | SEPT

Viola cornuta - *Horned pansy*

Violaceae
Violet family

Raponzolo orbicolare
Violette cornue

Found in damp meadows and woodland edges, V. cornuta (left) has fragrant flowers, usually pale lilac, with quite narrow petals, a white eye and a long spur behind. The two related species illustrated are Viola bubanii (right), with darker flowers and rounded petals, a yellow eye and a shorter spur and a pretty violet, Viola pyrenaica (inset), with heart shaped leaves and flowers with a white throat, white hairs and vertical purple stripes.

MAY | JUN | JUL | AUG | SEPT

Hepatica nobilis - Hepatica

| Ranunculaceae | Hierba de hígado |
| Buttercup family | Hépatique |

An early flowering woodland plant though surprisingly populations can also be found in the open high mountains, perhaps where there was formerly a shrub layer to shelter them. Three-lobed leaves often mottled with delightful patterns and delicate flowers of blue, white and occasionally pink.

MAY   JUN   JUL   AUG   SEPT

Lithospermum purpurocaerulea - *Blue gromwell*

Boraginaceae
Borage family

Mijo de sol de la flor azul
Grémil pourpre-bleu

A bushy plant of shady thickets and woodland edges on limestone with dark green pointed leaves and erect stems. Clusters of purplish-red buds open to the most glorious blue flowers followed by very tough, white seed capsules – its Latin name means 'stone seed'.

See Lithodora diffusa p36

MAY **JUN JUL AUG** SEPT

Scilla liliohyacinthus - Pyrenean squill

Asparagaceae
Asparagus family

Jacinto de bosque
Jacinthe des Pyrénées

A tall bulb that flowers early before the trees have come into leaf in, and at the edge of, deciduous woods. Large, shiny green leaves lie flat, above which rise stems with clusters of starry blue flowers.

See Scilla verna p27

MAY   JUN   JUL   AUG   SEPT

Gentianella campestris - Field gentian

Gentianaceae	Genciana de los campos
Gentian family	Gentiane champêtre

A biennial species with upward-pointing stems bearing oval leaves. Clusters of bluish-purple flowers, usually with four petals but occasionally five, even on the same flower stem. A delicate upward-pointing fringe surrounds and frames the white stamens.

MAY JUN JUL AUG SEPT

Iris latifolia - English iris

Iridaceae
Iris family

Lirio de montaña
Iris à larges feuilles

In Spring the tall, linear leaves of this spectacular flower emerge in huge numbers across the high meadows, followed by unmistakable flowers, usually vivid blue but occasionally white. Originates from the Pyrenees and Northern Spain but introduced into cultivation in England many centuries ago and then exported – hence the English name.

MAY JUN **JUL** **AUG** SEPT

Lithodora diffusa - *Scrambling gromwell*

| *Boraginaceae* | Carrasquilla azul |
| Borage family | Grémil diffus |

A plant endemic to the mountains of Northern Spain that seems almost ubiquitous in the Picos. Scrambling woody stems with hairy leaves carry clusters of vivid blue funnel-shaped flowers. Most common in woods and scrub but also thrives in high mountain locations and scree.

See Lithospermum purpurocaerulea p32

MAY   JUN   JUL   AUG   SEPT

Pinguicula grandiflora - *Large-flowered butterwort*

Lentibulariaceae	Grasilla
Butterwort family	Grassette à grandes fleurs

Found wherever there are bogs, wet rocks or slow-moving water. A carnivorous plant with sticky pale green leaves that trap small insects, a source of nutrients. Dark blue flowers with white throats.

MAY · JUN · JUL · AUG · SEPT

Gentiana alpina - *Southern gentian*

Gentianaceae	Genciana alpina
Gentian family	Gentiane des Alpes

Of several Trumpet gentian species in the European mountains, with subtle botanical differences, Gentiana alpina is the one commonly encountered in higher meadows on acid rocks in the Pyrenees. It has deep blue trumpets, spotted inside, but is best identified by its small oval, pale green leaves nearly as broad as long.

See Gentiana occidentalis p39

Gentiana occidentalis - *Pyrenean Trumpet Gentian*

Gentianaceae
Gentian family

Genciana occidental
Gentiane occidentale

This Trumpet gentian grows in high meadows and rocky places on limestone and is therefore often encountered in the Picos. Vivid blue trumpets rise above long pointed bright green leaves. The green sepal teeth (visible at the base of the petals) are distinctive, narrowing near their base, curving outwards above and culminating in a slightly curved point.

See Gentiana alpina p38

MAY   JUN   JUL   AUG   SEPT

Gentiana verna - *Spring gentian*

Gentianaceae	Genciana de primavera
Gentian family	Gentiane de printemps

The exquisite blue starry flowers of this early flowering Gentian sparkle in the turf and amidst the rocks of the high meadows, not long after the snow has melted. The flowers are held flat above a long narrow tube and bright green leaves forming a rosette at the base. Colour variation is sometimes found, from pale blue to purple. Surely little in the high mountains can challenge the beauty of this lovely flower?

MAY JUN JUL AUG SEPT

Globularia repens - *Creeping globularia*

| Globulariaceae | Arzolia |
| Globularia family | Globulaire naine |

A tiny plant that slowly creates the most compact mats over high limestone rocks, with leaves so tiny and pointed as to be prickly. An abundance of small, blue globe-shaped flowers cover the foliage, attracting bees and butterflies.

See Globularia nudicaulis p42

MAY **JUN** **JUL** AUG SEPT

Globularia nudicaulis - Leafless-stemmed globularia

Globulariaceae	Lluqueta nudicaule (Catalan)
Globularia family	Globulaire à tige nue

Single, blue globe-shaped flowers sit on elongated, leafless stems of this species found in rock crevices, rocky meadows and woodland edges. The leaves are dark green, fleshy and spoon-shaped.

See Globularia repens p41

Geranium pyrenaicum - Pyrenean cranesbill

Geraniaceae
Geranium family

Geranio pirenaico
Geranium des Pyrénées

Despite its name, a common species throughout Northern Europe in meadows, woodland edges and on wasteland. Low growing with round, deeply-cut leaves and pink or lilac flowers, petals notched at the ends.

MAY — JUN — JUL — AUG — SEPT

Horminum pyrenaicum - Dragonmouth

Lamiaceae	Toronjil de Roncevalles
Dead-nettle family	Hormin des Pyrénées

Upright stems carry purple flowers with open mouths above rosettes of round, fleshy leaves in woodland, meadows and high rocky places. The Spanish name means lemon balm from Roncevalles, an ancient town on a Pyrenean pilgrim route. The leaves are similar but not lemon-scented.

See Melittis melisophyllum p79, Muscari neglectum p46

MAY JUN JUL AUG SEPT

Muscari comosum - Tassel hyacinth

Liliaceae	Ajipuerco
Lily family	Muscari à toupet

A bulb with a most curious structure. At its top is a tassel of colourful violet-blue sterile flowers. Beneath are dark purple buds which open to brown downward-hanging flowers capable of producing seed. Widespread in rocky open ground and cultivated fields.

MAY   JUN   JUL   AUG   SEPT

Muscari neglectum - *Grape hyacinth*

Asparagaceae	Nazarenos
Asparagus family	Muscari à grappe

A dwarf bulb familiar in gardens where it can become a nuisance. In the wild it is found in rough open ground, roadsides and cultivated fields. Long grass-like leaves flat to the ground and dark purple flowers have a cluster of downward-facing bells and white mouths.

See Muscari comosum p45

MAY JUN JUL AUG SEPT

Orchis coriophora - Bug orchid

Orchidaceae
Orchid family

Clavellina
Orchis punaise

An uncommon small orchid whose Latin name means 'bug-bearing', a reference to its unpleasant scent. Dense, cylindrical flower spike. Flowers have an attractive white spotted lip edged with ruby red. Thrives in damp, even boggy, meadows.

MAY **JUN** **JUL** AUG SEPT

Orchis mascula - Early purple orchid

| Orchidaceae | Orquídea silvestre |
| Orchid family | Orchis mâle |

The most common early orchid found from lower meadows up to the high open mountains. The leaves often, but not always, have large brown blotches. The flower spikes are quite loose with variable flowers ranging from purple to pink. The sepals flare outwards and lip is white and spotted at the top with darker margins.

See Orchis morio p49

MAY JUN JUL AUG SEPT

Orchis morio - *Green-winged orchid*

Orchidaceae
Orchid family

Testículos de perro
Orchis bouffon

An early flowering orchid similar to Orchis mascula but distinguished by the upper sepals which form wings vertically striped, though not always green. The Spanish name describes the tubers from which it grows (perro means dog) while the French 'bouffon' means comical – the wings could perhaps represent a donkey's ears. Also named Anacamptis morio.

See Orchis mascula p48

| MAY | JUN | JUL | AUG | SEPT |

Orchis purpurea - *Lady orchid*

Orchidaceae	Orquídea purpura
Orchid family	Orchis pourpre

A large orchid, tall with broad, veined fleshy leaves. Dark-tipped buds open to form a purple hood, like a lady's bonnet, and a large lip supposedly shaped like a figure in a crinoline dress. Dry grassland on limestone. Not common but well worth finding. For contrast see the Man orchid and compare with the smaller Orchis ustulata.

See Orchis ustulata p51, Aceras anthropophorum p180

MAY | JUN | JUL | AUG | SEPT

Orchis ustulata - Burnt orchid

Orchidaceae	Orquídea manchada
Orchid family	Orchis brûlé

The dark colour of the unopened buds at the tip of the flowering spike of this orchid provides its name. Easily found in full sun in short grassland and mountain pastures, usually on limestone, and occasionally in open woodland or marshland. Also called Neotinea ustulata.

See Orchis purpurea p50

MAY   JUN   JUL   AUG   SEPT

Phyteuma charmelii - *Pyrenean rampion*

Campanulaceae
Bellflower family

Raponchigo
Raiponce de charmeil

Distinct from other similar species because of its round, not elongated, purple flower head and the long, toothed green bracts immediately below the flower. The name Rampion derives from the Latin name for a turnip – these species have fleshy roots, eaten in times past.

| MAY | JUN | JUL | AUG | SEPT |

Thymus serpyllum - *Wild thyme*

Lamiaceae
Dead nettle family

Serpol
Thym serpolet

A common and lovely creeping herb found on rocks, roadside and meadow edges. Elliptical flat fragrant green leaves and heads of purple flowers, very attractive to insects. Mediterranean species with small rounded leaves may also be encountered e.g. Thymus capitata (inset).

MAY | JUN | JUL | AUG | SEPT

Gentiana pyrenaica - Pyrenean gentian

Gentianaceae	Genciana pirenaica
Gentian family	Gentiane des Pyrénées

The striking purple, smaller trumpets of this Gentian make it quite distinct from the larger, bluer species that may grow with it in short turf in high meadows, particularly in moist or even boggy patches. Its small narrow leaves are often beneath the grass but its pure white stamens and anthers make it easily identified.

MAY **JUN** **JUL** **AUG** SEPT

Linaria alpina - Alpine toadflax

Scrophulariaceae
Figwort family

Violeta de glera
Linaire des Alpes

A low creeping plant of rocky places, screes and river gravels with grey-green leaves and prostrate stems carrying snapdragon flowers of shades of purple and blue. Usually an orange patch on the lower lip but forms exist with white throats or no colour variation. Contrast Linaria elegans (inset) that has similar flowers, without orange, on tall, thin stems.

See Linaria supina p135, Asarina procumbens p132, Antirrhinum majus p98

MAY JUN JUL AUG SEPT

Anacamptis pyramidalis - Pyramidal orchid

Orchidaceae
Orchid family

Orquídea piramidal
Orchis pyramidal

The flower spike of this orchid is pyramidal when it starts to open and elongates to form a delicate cylinder of small flowers, perhaps as many as 100 on a large specimen. Widespread in meadows on limestone and along roadsides, flowering after the earlier marsh orchids and extending the orchid season into the late summer.

MAY　JUN　JUL　AUG　SEPT

Anthyllis vulneraria ssp pyrenaica - Kidney vetch

| Fabiaceae | Vulneraria |
| Pea family | Anthyllide |

A ubiquitous species found at all levels and habitats from lowland meadows to the highest rocky screes. From scrambling mats of divided leaves covered in silky hairs rise clusters of flowers each with an even silkier calyx. In Northern Europe Kidney vetch almost always has yellow flowers. In the Pyrenees and Picos they are deep pink or red though, as shown, wide variation is found even in adjacent plants.

See Lotus corniculatus p108

Cardamine raphanifolia - *Radish-leaved bittercress*

Cruciferae
Cress family

Mastuerzo de hoja de rábano
Cardamine à larges feuilles

A robust cress, large stands of which are found in damp meadows and by streams, with oval leaves, the end leaf of each stem larger than the others. Heads of showy, four-petalled pink or violet flowers.

MAY   JUN   JUL   AUG   SEPT

Centranthus angustifolius - Narrow-leaved valerian

Valarianaceae
Valerian family

La Milamores
Centranthe à feuilles étroites

Grows in rocky places, walls, crevices and on roadsides in the Northern Spanish mountains, usually on limestone. Its height depends on altitude but upright stems bear blue-green pointed leaves with small leaves at each node. They carry loose clusters of pink flowers, each with a long spur. A relative of the Mediterranean Red valerian, cultivated and growing wild in many parts of the world.

Dactylorhiza elata - *Robust marsh orchid*

Orchidaceae	Satirion bastardo
Orchid family	Orchis élevé

As its name suggests, a tall, handsome inhabitant of wet, marshy meadows and streamsides. Its leaves are erect and not spotted. The flowers, in tall narrow spikes, are variable both in size and colour, ranging from deep purple to delicate pink, a fine sight when massed together.

See Dactylorhiza fuchsii p62, Dactylorhiza sambucina p63, Orchis mascula p48

MAY   JUN   JUL   AUG   SEPT

Dactylorhiza fuchsii - Common spotted marsh orchid

Orchidaceae
Orchid family

Orquídea de largas bractéas
Orchis de Fuchs

The most common and numerous marsh orchid, found in thousands in favourable locations in wet meadows, flowering after the early snowmelt species. Very variable in height and structure but usually with thin, elongated spotted leaves and a narrow flower spike with endless variations of stripes and spots, from deep pink to white.

See Dactylorhiza elata p61, Orchis mascula p48, Dactylorhiza sambucina p63

Dactylorhiza sambucina - *Elder-flowered orchid*

Orchidaceae
Orchid family

Orquídea con olor a sauco
Orchis sureau

Delicately scented of elder, this marsh orchid is unusual because its two strikingly different colour forms are often found side by side, sometimes with curious mixtures of the two. A robust and squat species with unspotted leaves and plump, compact flower spikes, often in large numbers in early wet meadows.

See Dactylorhiza elata p61, Dactylorhiza fuchsii p62, Orchis mascula p48

MAY   JUN   JUL   AUG   SEPT

Geranium sanguineum - *Bloody cranesbill*

| *Geraniaceae* | Geranio |
| Geranium family | Géranium rouge sang |

Forms a loose mat of hairy stems and divided green leaves in meadows, woodland edges and high rocky places. Vibrant purple flowers with white centres. The name derives from the red colour of the leaves in autumn and the long pointed seed pod, like a crane's bill.

Gymnadenia conopsea - Fragrant orchid

Orchidaceae	Caparrosa
Orchid family	L'orchis moucheron

A common and lovely orchid found in meadows, woodland edges and rocky places with narrow, unspotted green leaves. The flower spike is cylindrical with closely clustered, deliciously fragrant, pink flowers.

MAY   JUN   JUL   AUG   SEPT

Linum viscosum - *Sticky flax*

Linaceae	Lino viscoso
Flax family	Lin visqueux

As its name suggests, a plant with slightly sticky and hairy leaves above which rise clusters of large and flamboyant pink flowers. Lower meadows and grassy places.

See Linum narbonense p25

MAY   JUN   JUL   AUG   SEPT

Onobrychis argentea - Silvery sainfoin

| Fabiaceae | Pimpirigallo |
| Pea family | Sainfoin |

A tall sainfoin (literally 'healthy hay') found in dry rocky places on limestone. The upright flower spikes carry delicate vertical red stripes on a silvery-pink background. The soft, downy leaflets are silver beneath, hence the name.

MAY JUN JUL AUG SEPT

Ophrys apifera - Bee orchid

Orchidaceae	Orquídea abeja
Orchid family	Ophrys abeille

An orchid of grassland, scrub, and roadsides on limestone. The complex and colourful flowers mimic the appearance of a bumblebee but are usually self-pollinated. Grey-green strap-like leaves and a loose spike of flowers, the colours and patterns of which can be very variable and worth close study.

See other Ophrys species p182, p183, p70

Ophrys tenthredinifera - Sawfly orchid

Orchidaceae
Orchid family

Orquídea avispo
Ophrys guêpe

Surely the most flamboyant of the bee orchids but also infinitely variable in colour and pattern. Large brightly coloured flowers with bright pink sepals and large furry lips, usually edged in yellow. A colony in flower in sunshine is a most arresting sight.

See other Ophrys species p68, p182, p183

MAY JUN JUL AUG SEPT

Orchis papilionacea - Pink butterfly orchid

Orchidaceae
Orchid family

Orquídea mariposa
Orchis papillon

This unmistakable and colourful orchid is found, sometimes in significant numbers, in full sun on well-drained poor grassland and rocky places, usually on limestone. Note with pleasure the subtle variations in the pink lines and blotches on the lip. Also known as Anacamptis papilionaceae.

MAY JUN JUL AUG SEPT

Polygala comosa - *Tufted milkwort*

| *Polygalaceae* | Lechera |
| Milkwort family | Polygala chevelu |

A delicate plant with upright stems bearing long pointed leaves. Pink flowers with slightly lighter stamens protruding. Like all milkworts the flowers repay careful study of their unusual structure. Two sepals at the side form 'wings' with three smaller sepals behind. Three petals are joined at the base, the lowest being a boat shaped 'keel'.

See Polygala alpestris p26

Cephalanthera rubra - Red helleborine

Orchidaceae
Orchid family

Eleborine roja
Céphalanthère rouge

An elegant and beautiful woodland species with long, thin and pointed leaves. Loose spikes of bright pink flowers, which do not fully open, have a lip with a white centre and yellow markings.

MAY   JUN   JUL   AUG   SEPT

Daboecia cantabrica - *St Daboec's heath*

Ericaceae
Heather family

Brezo cantabrico
Bruyère de saint Daboec

A rambling shrub with dark green narrow leaves and large, rosy-pink flowers in loose clusters at the top of red stems. Found on heaths and woodland edges. Grows in the coastal areas of north-west Europe and is named after an early Irish saint.

Erica australis - *Spanish heath*

Ericaceae
Heather family

Brezo rojo
Bruyère

A tall but slender shrub with vibrant pink tubular, not bell-shaped, flowers in clusters at the top of vertical stems bearing upward-pointing bright green leaves. The darker anthers protrude from the scalloped flowers, a most attractive colour combination.

| MAY | JUN | JUL | AUG | SEPT |

Erythronium dens canis - Dog's tooth violet

Liliaceae
Lily family

Diente de perro
Dent de chien

The name of this plant derives from its bulb, shaped like a dog's canine. Most commonly found in dappled shade but populations also grow in grassy places high on the open mountains. Fleshy, mottled leaves and pretty flowers with reflexed petals in a variety of colours, pink, white and blue.

Melittis melissophyllum - Bastard balm

Labiate	Melisa bastarda
Mint family	Mélitte de feuilles de mélisse

A tall plant of woodland edges and glades, stems covered in white hairs and very aromatic leaves similar in appearance, but not scent, to the culinary herb Lemon balm – hence the name. The flowers are usually white with a patterned pink lower lip but entirely pink forms can be found.

MAY   JUN   JUL   AUG   SEPT

Ramonda myconi - Ramonda

Gesneriaceae
Gloxinia family

Oreja de oso
Ramonde des Pyrénées

A species endemic to, and one of the great joys of, the Pyrenees. Related to the tropical African Violets widely grown as house plants. Flourishes in damp shady rock crevices, where fleshy, wrinkled leaves, green above and rusty brown below form flat rosettes. Violet- blue flowers, sometimes slightly pink, rise singly or in small clusters with protruding yellow anthers. The Spanish name means 'bear's ear'.

MAY | JUN | JUL | AUG | SEPT

Valeriana montana - *Mountain valerian*

Valerianaceae	Valeriana de monte
Valerian family	Valériane des montagnes

Valerian species can be difficult to identify but this attractive plant, with pretty clusters of pink flowers, has upper leaves that are oval, toothed at the edge and not divided. Usually in damp shade on limestone, often in rock crevices.

Carduus carlinoides - Pyrenean thistle

Asteraceae
Daisy family

Cardo pirenaico
Chardon fausse carline

This formidably prickly thistle grows only in the Pyrenees and Northern Spain. Stems coated with white downy hairs carry leaves armed with sharp spines. Clusters of pink or slightly purple flowers, also surrounded by needles, rise attractively in grassy meadows and stony screes up into the high mountains.

MAY   JUN   JUL   AUG   SEPT

Daphne cneorum - *Garland flower*

Thymelaceae	Almezerion bajo
Thyme family	Daphné camelée

A lovely dwarf shrub that forms prostrate mats in limestone rocky meadows. Green pointed leaves at the end of woody stems, from which open clusters of delightfully fragrant flowers. Deep red buds open to various shades of pink. Flowering in very early Spring is a taller relative, Daphne mezereum, Mezereon, (inset) which later has orange berries.

MAY JUN JUL AUG SEPT

Helianthemum nummularium ssp pyrenaicum - Pyrenean rockrose

Cistaceae	Tamarilla
Rockrose family	Hélianthème commun

This sub-species of the Common Rockrose grows only in the Pyrenees and is worthy of separate illustration because of its beautiful flat pink flowers with contrasting yellow stamens and anthers. Woody stems, oval leaves and buds covered in glistening white hairs.

See Helianthemum nummularium p121, Helianthemum apenninum p142

MAY **JUN** **JUL** **AUG** SEPT

Erinus alpinus - *Fairy foxglove*

Scrophulariaceae
Figwort family

Erino
Erine des Alpes

A common but delicate and pretty plant that seeds itself into walls, cliffs, screes and crevices. Short stems carry clusters of bright flowers, usually purple but sometimes more pink. Widely in cultivation where it can be a nuisance and rather coarse. In the wild it is a joy to behold.

MAY JUN JUL AUG SEPT

Mathiola fruticulosa - *Sad stock*

Cruciferae
Cress family

Alhelí de campo
Matthiole en buisson

Compact grey-green, elongated leaves and bright pink flowers, with a creamy yellow eye, that are slightly fragrant. In high limestone screes and rock crevices forms a very compact and lovely plant but may be taller at lower altitudes. English name comes from a Latin alternative – M. tristis.

Pedicularis verticillata - Whorled Lousewort

Scrophulariaceae
Figwort family

Gorbiza de hojas en verticilos
Pédiculaire verticillée

A semi parasite, like Yellow rattle, that has its own roots but also lives on roots of coarse grasses. Several species with pink flowers can be difficult to distinguish but this has finely divided leaves in whorls of four with compact spikes of flowers which do not have the elongated beak of some species. Wet high meadows.

MAY **JUN** **JUL** AUG SEPT

Petrocallis pyrenaica - Pyrenean whitlow-grass

| Brassicaceae | Petrocallis |
| Cabbage family | Petrocallis des Pyrénées |

A lovely high mountain cushion plant of screes and rock crevices, usually on limestone but also on shale as shown. Rosettes of green elongate leaves form tight mats above which rise short stems covered in white hairs and four-petalled flowers with yellow anthers.

JUN JUL AUG

Petrocoptis pyrenaica - Petrocoptis

Caryophyllaceae
Pink family

Rompepiedras
Lychnis des Pyrénées

A number of sub-species of Petrocoptis, all endemic to the Pyrenees and Northern Spain, have minor botanical differences. All grow in shady, vertical rock crevices (its name means 'stone breaker') and have grey-green, succulent leaves on dangling stems. Flowers vary from white to pale pink to a lovely deep rose colour.

MAY JUN JUL AUG SEPT

Primula hirsuta - *Hirsute primrose*

Primulaceae
Primrose family

Primavera con pelos
Primevère hérissée

The leaves of this lovely plant are not prominently hairy, despite its name, but are fleshy and sticky with edges prominently toothed. Short stems carry clusters of reddish-pink flowers with a white eye. Rock crevices, usually with some shade, on acid rocks.

MAY — **JUN** — **JUL** — AUG — SEPT

Saponaria ocymoides - *Rock soapwort*

Caryophyllaceae
Pink family

Jabonera rastrera
Saponaire des rochers

A common plant on sunny, rocky areas and cliffs, particularly on roadsides, but rarely found in the higher mountains. Sprawling stems with oval leaves cloak the rocks covered with eye-catching mats of bright pink flowers.

MAY   JUN   JUL   AUG   SEPT

Silene acaulis - Moss campion

| Caryophyllaceae | Silene sin tallo |
| Pink family | Silène acaule |

A high mountain species that thrives on screes and rocks, forming tight, hard cushions of tiny green leaves. It covers itself with stemless pink flowers, so colourful that a large specimen is visible for a considerable distance. One of the most widespread of all mountain plants, growing around the Earth's entire Northern Hemisphere.

MAY JUN JUL AUG SEPT

Trifolium alpinum - Alpine clover

Fabiaceae	Regaliz de Puerto
Pea family	Trèfle alpin

This Clover, with its large and flamboyant upward-pointing pink flowers, makes prostrate carpets on high rocks, screes and pastures. Three leaves folded down the centre, from which the name is derived, grow from short stems that creep across rough, stony areas and through short grass. Usually grows on acid rocks.

See Vicia pyrenaica p97

Vicia pyrenaica - Pyrenean vetch

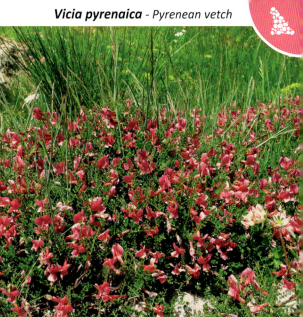

Fabiaceae
Pea family

Arveja pirenaica
Vesce des Pyrénées

A low-growing, loose mat with up to six pairs of leaflets and a twisting tendril. Vibrant pea flowers vary from deep crimson to bluish-purple to form a striking display on the high rocks and screes.

See Trifolium alpinum p96

MAY   JUN   JUL   AUG   SEPT

Antirrhinum majus - *Common snapdragon*

Scrophulariaceae
Figwort family

Boca de dragon
Muflier à grandes fleurs

A tall, unmissable and unmistakable flower of rocky limestone, roadsides and screes. Vivid purple-red flowers with white throats open as if they were the mouths of dragons. Yellow forms are also found.

See Linaria supina p135, Asarina procumbens p132

Nigritella nigra - *Vanilla orchid*

Orchidaceae	Estrella negra
Orchid family	Orchis vanille

A tiny orchid, colonies of which are dotted across high meadows. The pyramidal bud opens to a round star-like head of exquisite small flowers (Estrella means star). Usually dark red but lovely pink forms too, all deliciously scented of vanilla and chocolate.

MAY **JUN** **JUL** **AUG** SEPT

Serapias cordigera - *Heart-flowered orchid*

Orchidaceae	Gallos acorazonados
Orchid family	Serapias en Coeur

The largest of the tongue orchids and found in substantial numbers in damp meadows, near running water and on roadsides. The flowers are silver in bud and open to produce a long heart-shaped tongue, reddish-brown with darker veins and chocolate bristles at the throat.

See Serapias lingua p102, Serapias parviflora p103

Serapias lingua - *Tongue orchid*

| *Orchidaceae* | Gallos |
| Orchid family | Serapias langue |

The most common of the tongue orchids, found in meadows, scrub and on roadsides. A loose spike of silver buds opens to produce a succession of reddish-violet tongues with paler throats and fine hairs.

See Serapias cordigera p101, Serapias parviflora p103

MAY JUN JUL AUG SEPT

Serapias parviflora - Small-flowered tongue orchid

Orchidaceae	Gallos de flor peqûena
Orchid family	Serapias à petites fleurs

The smallest of the Tongue orchids, only a fraction of the height of Serapias cordigera, it is less common and not so visible in the damp grassy meadows. It has a quiet charm with small hooded flowers bearing a reddish tongue with a pale throat.

See Serapias cordigera p101, Seraoias lingua p102

MAY **JUN** JUL AUG SEPT

Vaccinium myrtillus - Bilberry

Ericaceae	Arandano
Heather family	Myrtille

A familiar plant of moors and open woodlands throughout northern Europe with edible purple berries in Autumn. Also, as shown, grows in shady rock crevices. Light green leaves on darker stems with small rounded pink and green nodding flowers.

MAY   JUN   JUL   AUG   SEPT

Pulsatilla rubra ssp hispanica - Dark pasque flower

Ranunculaceae
Buttercup family

Flor de viento
Pulsatille rouge

A special flower that grows only in the Picos and surrounding mountains on high limestone pastures. It has the darkest colour of any Pasque flower, appearing almost black unless viewed with the sun behind when its true dark red colour is seen. Unpalatable to cattle so survives in grazed land, but very uncommon and a joy to find.

Allium moly - *Yellow onion*

| *Amaryllidaceae* | Cebolleta, Suspiros del sol |
| Amaryllis family | Ail doré |

This colourful, widely cultivated onion illuminates dry, rocky places, particularly along roadsides where it can be seen in quantity. Heads of golden-yellow flowers rise above broad grey-green leaves. Edible and used in herbal medicine. Moly is a mythical drug used by Odysseus in Homer's Odyssey, to resist Circe's magic. The alternative Spanish name means 'sighs of the sun'.

MAY **JUN** **JUL** AUG SEPT

Caltha palustris - *Marsh marigold*

Ranunculaceae
Buttercup family

Hierba centella
Populage des marais

This plant, which grows in wet or boggy areas and at the edges of running water, is familiar throughout Northern Europe. It is found from the lower meadows, where it forms robust stands, to the highest mountain streams, where its height is much diminished. Large, shiny leaves on fleshy stems carry numerous open yellow goblets, sometimes tinged slightly orange.

MAY · JUN · JUL · AUG · SEPT

Lotus corniculatus - Bird's foot trefoil

| Fabiaceae | Zapaticos de Virgen |
| Pea family | Lotier corricule |

A very common species in lower meadows, on roadsides, woodland edges and high rocky places. Always vibrant and beautiful, colour variation is particularly striking in the Picos. Buds are often red and flowers normally yellow but a variety of orange and mixed shades delight the eye. Lotus alpinus is smaller and forms prostrate mats on rocks in high places. The Spanish name means 'Slippers of the Virgin'. See Anthyllis vulneraria p58

MAY JUN JUL AUG SEPT

Dactylorhiza insularis - Barton's orchid

Orchidaceae	Orquídea amarilla
Orchid family	Dactylorhize de Corse

A pale yellow orchid found in open woodland and meadows. Similar to the yellow form of Dactylorhiza sambucina, it differs by having narrower, more upright leaves, a looser, more cylindrical flower spike and, usually, two distinctive reddish-brown dots at the base of the lip.

See Dactylorhiza sambucina p63

| MAY | JUN | JUL | AUG | SEPT | |

Papaver cambrica - *Welsh poppy*

Papaveraceae
Poppy family

Amapola amarilla
Pavot de Pays de Galles

A yellow poppy that has escaped from cultivation in some parts of the world to become a nuisance but a real beauty in its natural habitat. Tall, with large showy flowers of bright yellow or orange at all altitudes on roadsides, woodland edges and high rocky places. Former name Meconopsis cambrica.

MAY **JUN** **JUL** **AUG** SEPT

Rhinanthus species - Yellow rattle

Scrophulariaceae	Pitinos
Figwort family	Rhinanthe

There are a number of species of Yellow rattle, not easy to distinguish, but all semi-parasites – they have their own roots but also live on coarse grasses. This assists other flowering plants to thrive, making them a key inhabitant of diverse hay meadows. All have yellow flowers with a downward pointing beak that may be vivid blue. When ripe the seeds rattle in their pods if shaken.

MAY **JUN** **JUL** **AUG** SEPT

Trollius europaeus - *Globe flower*

Ranunculaceae	Calderones
Buttercup family	Trolle d' Europe

A widespread resident of wet grassland both in the lower meadows, where it is tall and stately, and higher where its height diminishes. The lovely yellow globes (the Spanish name means 'cauldron') remain closed but small insects creep inside to pollinate them.

| MAY | JUN | JUL | AUG | SEPT |

Chamaespartium sagittale - Winged broom

Fabiaceae	Carquexia fina
Pea family	Genêt ailé

A low-growing Broom readily identified by its upward-pointing yellow flowers on vertical stems, with winged ridges reminiscent of an arrow with its fletchings. Sagitta means arrow in Latin. Scrambles through rocky limestone areas usually in dappled shade.

MAY JUN JUL AUG SEPT 113

Cypripedium calceolus - Lady's slipper orchid

Orchidaceae	Zapatilla de dama
Orchid family	Sabot de Vénus

A truly spectacular orchid only a small population of which grows in the Spanish Pyrenees. They are kept under guard when in flower and, because their environment is protected, are slowly multiplying. Unmistakable, with strongly veined, pointed leaves. The flowers have deep reddish-brown sepals and petals and a yellow slipper-shaped lip marked with orange dots.

MAY   JUN   JUL   AUG   SEPT

Gentiana lutea - Great yellow gentian

Gentianaceae
Gentian family

Xanzaina
Gentiane jaune

Not all Gentians are blue. This tall inhabitant of woodland edge and dappled shade has whorled clusters of bright yellow flowers ascending on a robust stem above pointed bluish-green leaves. The plant illustrated is subspecies montserratii which has particularly large and flamboyant flowers. The roots are used not only for medicinal purposes but also to flavour alcoholic drinks.

MAY **JUN** **JUL** **AUG** SEPT

Lonicera etrusca - Etruscan honeysuckle

Caprifoliaceae
Honeysuckle family

Madreselva etrusca
Chèvrefeuille d'Etrurie

A climbing shrub that can reach a considerable height, scrambling and twining through trees and over scrub and rocky ground. It carries large, gloriously fragrant flower clusters of creamy yellow and reddish purple. A honeysuckle found throughout the Mediterranean lands.

Gagea nevadensis - Pyrenean gagea

Liliaceae	Estrella amarilla
Lily family	Étoile jaune

A dwarf bulb of high mountain pastures and woodland edges. Grassy, green pointed leaves and upward-facing flowers (the Spanish and French names means 'yellow star').

MAY **JUN** JUL AUG SEPT

Genista hystrix - Hedgehog gorse

Fabiaceae
Pea family

Erizon leones
Ajonc

One of many yellow-flowered gorses and brooms in the Pyrenees and Northern Spain, often very difficult to distinguish. This compact, spiny species covers limestone rocks and screes, its stems bearing upward-facing narrow leaves with hairs beneath and clusters of bright yellow flowers. Hystrix is a family of animals including the porcupine while erizo is Spanish for hedgehog – the English name given is a literal translation.

MAY	JUN	JUL	AUG	SEPT

Geum montanum - *Alpine avens*

Rosaceae	Cariofilada de montana
Rose family	Benoîte des montagnes

A common inhabitant of mountain meadows with flat green leaves with a large end leaflet. The flowers are upward-facing and bright yellow, followed by distinctive seed heads like twisted reddish tassels.

MAY · JUN · JUL · AUG · SEPT

Helianthemum nummularium - *Common rockrose*

Cistaceae	Tamarilla
Rockrose family	Héliantheme commun

A very common and showy plant found in rocky, dry places at all altitudes usually on limestone. Woody stems carry oval leaves and colourful flowers, usually yellow but sometimes orange or white.

See Helianthemum apennininum p142, Helianthemum nummularium ssp pyrenaicum p86

Hieracium mixtum ssp bombycinum - Bumblebee hawkweed

Asteraceae
Daisy family

Pelosilla blanca
Epervière mixte

Endemic to the mountains of Northern Spain and the Western Pyrenees this is a gem in a family that is not without its weeds. Deliciously hairy round green leaves and stems – bombycinum means 'bumblebee'. Delicate yellow dandelion flowers. Crevices in limestone.

Lilium pyrenaicum - Yellow Turk's Cap Lily

Liliaceae
Lily family

Azucena del Pirineo
Lis des Pyrénées

A lily found only in the Pyrenees and Northern Spain with upward-pointing narrow green leaves all along its tall stem. Yellow petals with dark spots curl upwards, like a turban, with contrasting orange anthers. Grows on rocky mountainsides and in steep, rough meadows, sometimes in large colonies.

MAY **JUN** **JUL** AUG SEPT

Narcissus abscissus - Trumpet daffodil

| *Amaryllidaceae* | Narciso |
| Amaryllis family | Narcisse |

A large daffodil with a bright yellow trumpet which forms a straight, not flared, tube in contrast to N. nobilis. 'Abscissus' means 'cut off'. The petals are usually paler yellow and tend to droop forward slightly.

See Narcissus asturiensis p125, Narcissus nobilis p126

MAY JUN JUL AUG SEPT

Narcissus asturiensis - *Asturian daffodil*

Amaryllidaceae	Narciso de Asturias
Amaryllis family	

An exquisite, tiny daffodil, a miniature of the many large cultivars grown in gardens. Found only in north-east Spain, it is a snowmelt plant, among the first to flower in the high limestone meadows. Its delicate, flared yellow trumpets nod gently forward.

See Narcissus abscissus p124, Narcissus nobilis p126

MAY **JUN** JUL AUG SEPT

Narcissus nobilis leoninus - *Leon daffodil*

| *Amaryllidaceae* | Trompon leones |
| Amaryllis family | Narcisse des prés |

A splendid large daffodil with a bright yellow trumpet that flares at the mouth and contrasting pale petals behind, the colour of which deepens at the base. The form illustrated is particularly large and grows in the Spanish province of Leon. Flowers early in moist mountain meadows, often in huge numbers particularly in the Picos – a glorious spectacle.

See Narcissus abscissus p124, Narcissus asturiensis p125

Narcissus triandrus - *Angel's tears daffodil*

Amaryllidaceae	Narciso con tres estambres
Amaryllis family	Jonquille blanche

Frequently encountered, but rarely in large numbers, among shrubs and light woodland on rocky hillsides. This very small distinctive daffodil has two or three pendulous creamy yellow flowers with upward-sweeping petals. The botanical name derives from the three anthers that protrude from the base of the delicate trumpet and the Spanish name given is a translation of this. The English name is surely more poetic.

Primula elatior - Oxlip

Primulaceae
Primrose family

Primavera comun
Primevère élevée

An early flowering, larger relative of the Cowslip (elatior means 'taller'), often found in abundance in wet meadows and by streams just after the snow has melted. Heads of pale yellow flowers with darker centres rise from fleshy, crinkled leaves.

MAY · JUN · JUL · AUG · SEPT

Adonis pyrenaica - Pyrenean pheasant's eye

Ranunculaceae	Adonis de los Pirineos
Buttercup family	L'Adonis des Pyrénées

An uncommon and lovely species endemic to the high Pyrenees. In wild rocky places emerge feathery, finely-cut green leaves and large yellow goblets with shiny golden petals, which rapidly flower and wither away. Named after the beautiful lover of the goddess Aphrodite in Greek myth. Killed by a wild boar, she poured nectar where his blood was spilt and an exquisite flower grew.

MAY **JUN** **JUL** AUG SEPT

Androsace vitaliana - *Vitaliana*

Primulaceae	Gregoria
Primrose family	Androsace de vital

A plant of high, exposed acid rocks and screes that forms extensive loose mats both in full sun and shady crevices. It has rosettes of grey-green needle-like leaves that are almost completely obscured by stemless bright gold flowers, a glorious sight when in full bloom.

MAY | JUN | JUL | AUG | SEPT

Asarina procumbens - Creeping snapdragon

Scrophulariaceae	Asarina
Figwort family	Asarine couchée

In lower locations this creeping Snapdragon can form trailing mats with sticky leaves and long stems. In the high mountains it inhabits tight crevices, usually in deep shade, its gaping cream and yellow flowers, with pink stripes and spots, reaching out like fledgling birds waiting to be fed.

See Linaria supina p135, Linaria alpina p55, Anirrhinum majus p98

MAY JUN JUL AUG SEPT

Echinospartum horridum - *Echinospartum*

Fabiaceae
Pea family

Erizon
Genêt horrible

This tight, low shrub grows in dense mats, often covering large areas of limestone rocky slopes and screes. Extremely spiny with pairs of vibrant flowers turning entire hillsides yellow.

See Genista hystrix p119

MAY   JUN   JUL   AUG   SEPT

Erysimum duriaei - Treacle mustard

Cruciferae
Cress family

Erismo de roquedos
Vélar des Pyrénées

A species found only in Northern Spain but with similar relatives throughout Europe. Growing in limestone crevices and screes, stems with many narrow upward-pointing green leaves carry a mass of bright yellow, four-petalled mustard flowers.

Linaria supina - Pyrenean toadflax

Scrophulariaceae
Figwort family

Mosquitas de los Pirineos
Linaire couchée

A slightly larger relative of Linaria alpina, found only in and around the Pyrenees and Picos. It scrambles through rocky places, wasteland and roadsides and has upright heads of flowers with long spurs. The upper petals are white, the lower pale yellow at the edge turning ever deeper in colour into the flowers' throat.

See Linaria alpina p55, Asarina procumbens p132, Antirrinhum majus p98

MAY JUN JUL AUG SEPT

Saxifraga aretioides - *Yellow saxifrage*

| *Saxifragaceae* | Rompepiedras amarillo |
| Saxifrage family | Saxifrage de burser |

A lovely crevice plant, unique to Pyrenees and Northern Spain, growing on shady vertical clefts in limestone. Tight cushions of tiny grey-green rosettes, above which branched stems with small green leaves bear clusters of rich yellow flowers.

MAY · **JUN** · **JUL** · AUG · SEPT

Orobanche species - Broomrape

Orobanchaceae	Orobanche
Broomrape family	Orobanche

A complicated plant family of parasitic species that live wholly on the roots of a host, for example Broom – hence the English name. Flower spikes are a variety of colours, all with gaping, somehow unsettling flowers. Found in all habitats from lowland meadows and roadsides to high mountain rocky terrain.

MAY   JUN   JUL   AUG   SEPT

Fritillaria pyrenaica - Pyrenean fritillary

Liliaceae	Corona imperial
Lily family	Fritillaire des Pyrénées

Flowering soon after the snow melts on the high mountain slopes, carpets of this distinctive small bulb can be a very arresting sight. Delicate nodding bells of purplish-brown, streaked with green or yellow. Be sure to lift the flower to study the inside, chequered in a variety of those same colours.

MAY JUN JUL AUG SEPT

Euphrasia alpina - Alpine eyebright

| Scrophulariaceae | Eufrasia de Asturias |
| Figwort family | Euphraise des Alpes |

A semi-parasite which has its own roots but also lives on the roots of host plants. Short stems with green, toothed leaves and delicate white flowers, the lower petals having a yellow throat and vertical markings, the upper petals purple or pink.

Filipendula vulgaris - Dropwort

Rosaceae
Rose family

Filipendula alba
Spirée filipendule

A plant of dry meadows on limestone with finely-cut fern-like leaves and pretty heads of pink buds opening to white flowers. It has no fragrance, unlike its taller relative Filipendula ulmaria, Meadowsweet, which inhabits wet meadows and marshes.

MAY   JUN   JUL   AUG   SEPT

Helianthemum apenninum - *White rockrose*

| Cistaceae | Rosa de las rocas blanca |
| Rockrose family | Héliantème des Apennins |

An inhabitant of rocky, grassy locations and roadsides on limestone with woody stems and long, thin leaves, hairy beneath, with edges slightly rolled over. Clusters of large white flowers with yellow centres and yellow stamens.

See Helianthemum nummularium p121, H. nummularium pyrenaicum p86

MAY **JUN** **JUL** **AUG** **SEPT**

Himantoglossum hircinum - Lizard orchid

Orchidaceae
Orchid family

Orquídea hedionda
Orchis bouc

A startling orchid, that emerges from the ground as a plump conical bud surrounded by fleshy green leaves. Cylindrical cluster of greenish-cream flowers with pink markings and a very long twisted tongue that provides the English name. Strong-smelling - hircinum and bouc mean goat, hedionda means stinking. Grassy places, wasteland and roadsides, sometimes in large colonies.

MAY   JUN   JUL   AUG   SEPT

Platanthera chlorantha - Greater butterfly orchid

Orchidaceae
Orchid family

Platantera de montana
Platanthère à fleurs vertes

Found in open meadows and woodland this tall, very visible orchid has open spikes of white flowers held well away from the stem, with long downward-curving spurs behind and a long lip with a green tip.

MAY JUN JUL AUG SEPT

Reseda suffruticosa - Tall mignonette

Resedaceae
Mignonette family

Reseda mayor
Réséda

This dramatic plant of dry rough ground on limestone can reach as high as two metres. A rosette of very finely cut green leaves, from which rises a tall spike, with smaller side shoots, bearing exquisite white flowers with contrasting orange anthers that fade to cream as the flower fully opens.

Anemone nemorosa - Wood anemone

Ranunculaceae
Buttercup family

Anemona de bosque
Anémone des bois

A woodland flower widespread in ancient woodlands and plantations, often in close harmony with Erythronium dens-canis and Hepatica nobilis. Finely-divided green leaves carpet the woodland flower above which stand flowers with six petals in a lovely array of pastel colours from white, the most common, to pink and blue and with stamens of yellow or orange.

See Anemone pavoniana p150, Erythronium dens-canis p78, Hepatica nobilis p30

MAY   JUN   JUL   AUG   SEPT

Polygonatum multiflorum - *Common Solomon's seal*

Asparagaceae
Asparagus family

Sello de salomon
Sceau de Salomon multiflore

An elegant species of shady woodland with arching, rounded stems carrying reflexed leaves and hanging white unscented flowers. A relative P. odoratum with angled stems and larger, bell-shaped flowers is fragrant (inset). Long used in traditional medicine, the roots bear circular scars once the stems have died back, in the shape of a signet ring or seal.

MAY   JUN   JUL   AUG   SEPT

Prunus padus - Bird cherry

Rosaceae	Cerezo de racimos
Rose family	Cérisier à grappes

A small deciduous tree, found in woods but also in the mountains right up to the tree-line with typical cherry leaves and lovely, scented white blossom with yellow stamens. Small black fruit follow, unpalatable to humans but a food source for birds.

Anemone narcissiflora - *Narcissus-flowered anemone*

Ranunculaceae	Anemona de flores de narciso
Buttercup family	Anémone à fleurs de narcisse

A plant of the more sheltered high meadows with groups of five or more white flowers with contrasting yellow stamens radiating from a stem that rises above deeply-cut leaves. Similarity to a Narcissus is not easy to discern but the key difference from its relative Pulsatilla alpina is that the flowers of the latter are single and do not form clusters.

See Pulsatilla alpina p154

MAY **JUN** **JUL** AUG SEPT

Anemone pavoniana - *Cantabrian anemone*

Ranunculaceae
Buttercup family

Anemona de cantabrica

This delicate small Anemone grows only in the Cordillera Cantabrica and Western Pyrenees and is most easily located in the high rocky meadows of the Picos. It generally grows in sheltered, damp niches among small shrubs and low grasses. It has very finely-cut dark green leaves and single white flowers with yellow stamens, much smaller than Pulsatilla alpina, its altogether more robust relation.
See Pulsatilla alpina p154, Anemone nemorosa p146

| MAY | JUN | JUL | AUG | SEPT |

Asphodelus albus - *White asphodel*

Asphodelaceae	Gamon
Asphodel family	Asphodèle blanc

This dramatic and unmistakable plant abounds in the higher meadows and rocky places, sometimes covering whole hillsides with its stately strap-like leaves and tall flower spikes. The flowers open in sequence, from the base, white with prominent contrasting orange anthers.

MAY JUN JUL AUG SEPT

Cistus salvifolius - *Sage leaved cistus*

Cistaceae
Rockrose family

Jaguarzo morisco
Ciste à feuilles de sauge

A species common throughout the Mediterranean region that extends north to the Picos and Pyrenees. A low-growing shrub which creeps over rocks in dry, hot locations. Rough, sage-like leaves and large, showy flowers on long stalks with white petals, yellow at the base, and yellow stamens.

See Helianthemum apenninum p142

Erica arborea - Tree heather

Ericaceae
Heather family

Brezo blanco
Bruyère blanche

A large, dense shrub with numerous very tiny leaves and small white bell-shaped flowers in dense clusters with a sweet fragrance. Can cover hillsides on rough terrain and heaths, a fine sight in full flower.

See Erica australis p77

MAY   JUN   JUL   AUG   SEPT

Pulsatilla alpina - Alpine pasque flower

Ranunculaceae	Flor de viento
Buttercup family	Pulsatille des alpes

A beautiful inhabitant of high meadows and limestone rocks with large finely-cut leaves and upward-facing white flowers with a rich boss of yellow stamens. There is a less common, equally lovely, yellow form, P. alpina apiifolia (see inset) more often found on acid rocks.

See Pulsatilla vernalis p155, Anemone narcissifolia p149, Anemone pavoniana p150

MAY **JUN** **JUL** AUG SEPT

Pulsatilla vernalis - *Spring pasque flower*

Ranunculaceae	Pulsatilla de primavera
Buttercup family	Pulsatille de printemps

One of the first and loveliest of the high snowmelt flowers. In the Spring sunshine it opens its white goblets, the exterior purple or blue and cloaked in fine hairs, to reveal delicate yellow stamens within. Often found growing with purple Pulsatilla vulgaris (inset).

See Pulsatilla alpina p154

MAY **JUN** JUL AUG SEPT

Ranunculus aconitifolius - Aconite-leaved buttercup

Ranunculaceae
Buttercup family

Ranunculo con hoja de aconito
Renoncule à feuilles d'aconit

A tall buttercup often found in dense colonies in wet meadows, by running water and in woodland edges. Lower leaves are deeply-cut, above which rise branched clusters of white flowers, each quite small but in quantity an impressive display.

See Ranunculus amplexicaulis p157, Ranunculus pyrenaeus p159

Ranunculus amplexicaulis - Clasped-leaf buttercup

Ranunculaceae　　　　　　　　　　Ranunculo de hojas abrazadoras
Buttercup family　　　　　　　　　　Renoncule à feuilles embrassantes

One of several white buttercups, this species is found only in Northern Spain. Distinguished by its leaves which have stalks and are broad, veined and pointed. The stem leaves are clasped round the stem at their base. High, rocky meadows, often in large swathes.

See Ranunculus aconitifolius p156, Ranunculus pyrenaeus p159

MAY　　JUN　　JUL　　AUG　　SEPT

Ranunculus aquatilis - Common water crowfoot

Ranunculaceae	Ranunculo acuatico
Buttercup family	Renoncule aquatique

An aquatic plant that grows in ponds and slow-moving water. Flat divided leaves, perhaps like a crow's foot, float on the water while pale stems lift white buttercup flowers with yellow centres above the surface. Found at all altitudes but notably in permanently wet high meadows.

MAY JUN JUL AUG SEPT

Ranunculus pyrenaeus - Pyrenean buttercup

Ranunculaceae
Buttercup family

Ranunculo de los Pirineos
Renoncule des Pyrénées

A white buttercup of the high wet meadows and rocky places usually with single flowers rising above leaves which enable the species to be distinguished. They are bluish-green, very narrow, pointed and without stalks.

See Ranunculus aconitifolius p156, Ranunculus amplexicaulis p157

| MAY | JUN | JUL | AUG | SEPT |

Teesdaliopsis conferta - Teesdaliopsis

Cruciferae
Cabbage family

Endemic to the Picos and surrounding mountains this is a plant of high rocky meadows, often in partial shade. Related to Iberis (Candytuft) species it has rosettes of long, slender leaves and relatively tall stems and large heads of white four-petalled flowers.

See Iberis sempervirens p171, Iberis carnosa p170

MAY　JUN　JUL　AUG　SEPT

Teucrium pyrenaicum - *Pyrenean germander*

Labiatae
Mint family

Teucrio pirenaico
Germandrée des Pyrénées

A low, creeping plant with flat leaves, glossy above and hairy beneath. It forms rosettes against rocks and in dry waste areas on limestone. Each rosette carries an attractive cluster of purple buds that open to reveal a white lower lip, though frustratingly this occurs in sequence so the mat is rarely covered in bloom.

MAY   JUN   JUL   AUG   SEPT

Androsace vandellii - *Vandelli's rock jasmine*

Primulaceae	Androsace imbricada (Catalan)
Primrose family	Androsace de Vandelli

This classic high-mountain crevice plant forms tight, delicate cushions in sheltered overhangs in granite and other lime free cliffs. It is rarely found lower than 2000m and inhabits the loftiest and least accessible cliffs. Protected from rain and snow, tiny grey rosettes are covered with silky hairs from which emerge stemless white flowers with five petals and a yellow centre. A cushion covered with flowers, tiny though it may be, is a lovely sight.

MAY JUN JUL AUG SEPT

Androsace villosa - Hairy rock jasmine

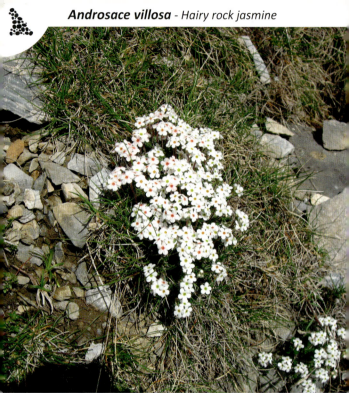

Primulaceae
Primrose family

Androsela pilosa
Androsace velue

A high-mountain plant that both creeps through turf in meadows on limestone and forms compact cushions in tight crevices. It has rosettes covered in fine hairs. Depending on habitat, flowers may be held close to the cushion or rise above the short grass on stems also silky with hairs. They have yellow centres that turn an attractive deep pink after pollination.

MAY **JUN** **JUL** AUG SEPT

Arenaria montana - Mountain sandwort

Caryophyllaceae
Pink family

Ala de mosca muerta
Sabline des montagnes

Large flowers with pure white petals and anthers adorn this species which forms loose mats of stems with narrow, pointed green leaves. Found growing in crevices and scree, often trailing vertically, usually on acid rocks.

Asperula hirta - Woodruff

Rubiaceae
Bedstraw family

Asperilla peluda
Aspérule hérissée

This species, endemic to the Pyrenees and mountains of Northern Spain, is found in cracks and fissures in limestone rocks. Its stems have whorls of six leaves with hairy edges that carry delicate and delightful pink buds. They open to form white four-petalled flowers. This plant is surely at its very best when partly in flower, the pink blending perfectly with the white.
See front cover.

MAY JUN JUL AUG SEPT

Cerastium alpinum - *Alpine mouse-ear*

Caryophyllaceae
Pink family

Oreja de raton de montana
Céraiste des Alpes

Forms large mats of creeping stems on rocks and screes which cover themselves with a carpet of pure white five-petalled flowers with each petal deeply notched on its outer edge.

Dryas octopetala - Mountain avens

Rosaceae
Rose family

Driade
Dryade à huit pétales

A classic high-mountain plant which carpets limestone rocks with its oak-like leaves (dryads were mythical nymphs of the oak forests) above which sit lovely white eight-petalled flowers with a boss of golden stamens.

MAY — **JUN** — **JUL** — AUG — SEPT

Iberis carnosa - *Spoon-leaved candytuft*

Cruciferae
Cabbage family

Carraspique cantabrica
L'ibéris spathule

A small plant of high rocks and screes, whose red stems carry spoon-shaped green leaves. Pink buds, tinged with purple-red, open first white and then a delicate lilac-pink, a very pleasing palette of colours. Also called I. spathulata.

See Iberis sempervirens p171, Teesdaliopsis conferta p160

Iberis sempervirens - *Evergreen candytuft*

Cruciferae
Cabbage family

Canasta de plata
L'ibéris toujours verte

Woody stems carry thick, oblong green leaves above which four-petalled white flowers form showy clusters. Grows on rocks and in screes in high places throughout the Mediterranean region but nevertheless an easy species in widespread garden cultivation.

See Iberis carnosa p170, Tessdaliopsis conferta p160

MAY   JUN   JUL   AUG   SEPT

Ranunculus parnassifolius - Parnassus buttercup

Ranunculaceae
Buttercup family

Ranunculo de glera
Renoncule à feuilles de parnassie

An inhabitant of high, wet screes and stream banks, this lovely buttercup usually has white flowers with yellow stamens above oval shiny leaves. In the Eastern Pyrenees, particularly on the high ridges above Nuria, grows the beautiful form shown with large goblets of white patterned with delicate pink - an example of how the most beautiful flowers often grow in the bleakest of locations.
See Ranunculus pyrenaeus p159, Ranunculus amplexicaulis p157

MAY **JUN** **JUL** AUG SEPT

Saxifraga canaliculata - *Mossy saxifrage*

Saxifragaceae
Saxifrage family

Saxifraga cantabrica

A vigorous species, endemic to the mountains of Northern Spain, which can form huge cushions over limestone rocks in the high mountains. Rosettes of divided sticky leaves bear quite tall stems with clusters of white flowers.

| MAY | JUN | JUL | AUG | SEPT |

Saxifraga conifera - Cone saxifrage

Saxifragaceae
Saxifrage family

A curious but attractive species, found only in the mountains of Northern Spain. Tiny conical silver and red buds, dormant in summer, carry fragile red stems with pretty white flowers. Grows in damp, partly shaded crevices on high limestone mountains.

MAY JUN JUL AUG SEPT

Saxifraga longifolia - Pyrenean saxifrage

Saxifragaceae
Saxifrage family

Corona de rey
Saxifrage à feuilles longues

A glory of Pyrenean limestone cliffs, the King's Crown in Spanish. Long leaved rosettes, with silver encrustation, grow in vertical crevices, taking many years to reach flowering size. They flower once only, producing a magnificent plume of white flowers, then die leaving many seeds, from some of which the next generation will emerge.

See rosette p13

MAY **JUN** **JUL** **AUG** SEPT

Saxifraga pubescens - *Hairy saxifrage*

Saxifragaceae
Saxifrage family

Rompepiedras pelosa
Saxifrage pubescente

Endemic to the Pyrenees, this Saxifrage forms tight cushions of slightly hairy and sticky rosettes. The best forms completely cover themselves in white flowers on short stems. Found on rocks of all types up to the highest summits.

Sedum album - White stonecrop

Crassulaceae
Stonecrop family

Uvas de perro
L'orpin blanc

Of the several Stonecrop species in the Pyrenees and Picos this is perhaps the most common and attractive. Clusters of small round succulent leaves (the Spanish name means 'Dog's grapes'), often tinged with red, carry starry white flowers. Rock crevices and walls.

MAY JUN JUL AUG SEPT

Aceras anthropophorum - Man orchid

Orchidaceae
Orchid family

Flor del hombre ahorcado
L'homme pendu

Widespread but not always easily spotted because of its muted colours, the flower spike of this orchid consists of numerous small flowers, usually yellow-green but sometimes a rich red. They are shaped like the body of a hanged man - hence Spanish and French names. Contrast their fate with the flowers of the Lady orchid!

See Orchis purpurea p50

MAY   JUN   JUL   AUG   SEPT

Cruciata laevipes - Crosswort

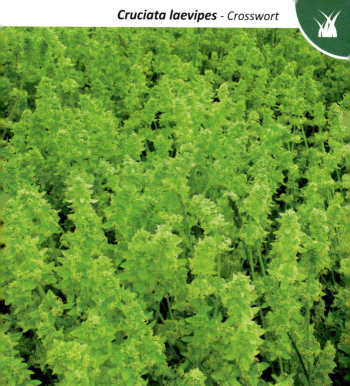

Rubiaceae
Bedstraw family

Creuera groga
Gaillet croisette

A creeping plant of scrub and wasteland on limestone with upright hairy stems carrying lime-green leaves and whorls of pale yellow sweet-scented flowers. As shown, may be the dominant species in such locations.

| MAY | JUN | JUL | AUG | SEPT |

Ophrys fusca - Dull ophrys / *O. insectifera*

Orchidaceae
Orchid family

Orquida abeja oscura
Ophrys brun

The muted colours of this bee orchid make it hard to spot but when found may be in quantity, with subtle variations to the green petals and chocolate lip with velvet hairs and vertical slate-silver bands. On the right is Ophrys insectifera, the Fly orchid, with diminutive flowers resembling flies (the Latin name means 'insect bearing) but pollinated by bees, deceived by its appearance into collecting pollen on their heads. Rocky grassland and roadsides. See other Ophrys species p68, p183

MAY   JUN   JUL   AUG   SEPT

Ophrys lutea - Yellow ophrys / *O. sphegodes*

Orchidaceae
Orchid family

Orquídea amarilla
Ophrys jaune

Usually a short species found in dry, rocky places, with greenish-yellow flowers bearing a broad, distinctive yellow margin around a brown centre on its lip. Shown on the right is Ophrys sphegodes, the Early spider orchid, the flower of which resembles the abdomen of a large hairy spider though it is pollinated by bees. These Ophrys species are infinitely variable in colour and pattern the careful observation of which gives great pleasure.

| MAY | JUN | JUL | AUG | SEPT |

Epipactis helleborine - Broad-leaved helleborine

Orchidaceae
Orchid family

Epipactis de hojas amplias
Epipactis à larges feuilles

An orchid of dry woodland in dappled shade with a tall stem carrying broad, pointed green leaves and a downward-curved spike of buds. The flowers when open bear delicate hairs and are variable in colour, usually greenish-yellow but occasionally suffused completely with pink and reddish-brown. Also shown on the right is E. microphylla, the small-leaved helleborine, similar but very miniature. Close study of its tiny flowers with a lens reveals their quiet beauty.

Helleborus viridis - Green hellebore

Ranunculaceae
Buttercup family

Eleboro verde
Ellébore vert

Dull green, palm-like leaves and upright stems with large, open green flowers and distinctive pointed seeds pods after pollination. The similar Helleborus foetidus, Stinking hellebore has more finely-divided leaves and smaller flowers with a red rim and an unpleasant scent. Woods and shady places in high pastures.

MAY JUN JUL AUG SEPT

Euphorbia amygdaloides - Wood spurge

Liliaceae
Lily family

Euforbio
L'Euphorbe des bois

This widespread species is found not only in woods, where it grows quite tall, but in dry places high in the open mountains where its distinctive red runners creep among the rocks and mountain flowers. Attractive sprays of yellow-green flowers and bracts are often tinged with orange, red and purple.

See Euphorbia flavicoma p187

MAY   JUN   JUL   AUG   SEPT

Euphorbia flavicoma - Yellow spurge

Euphorbiaceae
Spurge family

Bambollera
Euphorbe à têtes jaune d'or

A low-growing plant widespread in woodland glades and damp places with rounded green leaves. Heads of frothy bright yellow flowers and bracts rise above – the Spanish name means bubbly. Shown is ssp occidentalis, endemic to Northern Spain, but even more yellow forms are found through France and Spain.

See Euphorbia amygdaloides p186

MAY   JUN   JUL   AUG   SEPT

Sempervivum arachnoideum - Cobweb houseleek

Crassulaceae
Stonecrop family

Siempreviva de tela de araña
Joubarbe à toile d'araignée

Of a number of Sempervivum species this is the most distinctive, with tight rosettes in rock crevices each coated with white hairs like a spider's web. Stems carry clusters of bright pink flowers with yellow stamens after which the rosette dies to be replaced by small offsets from their neighbours.

Index - Latin

Aceras anthropophorum	180
Adonis pyrenaica	129
Allium moly	106
Anacamptis pyramidalis	56/57
Androsace vandellii	162/163
Androsace villosa	164/165
Androsace vitaliana	130/131
Anemone narcissiflora	149
Anemone nemorosa	146
Anemone pavoniana	150
Anthyllis vulneraria (ssp)	58
Antirrhinum majus	98/99
Aquilegia pyrenaica	18
Arenaria montana	166
Asarina procumbens	132
Asperula hirta	167
Asphodelus albus	151
Brimeura amethystina	19
Caltha palustris	107
Campanula patula	20
Cardamine raphanifolia	59
Carduncellus mitissimus	21
Carduus carlinensis	83
Centranthus angustifolius	60
Cephalanthera rubra	75
Cerastium alpinum	168
Chamaespartium sagittale	113
Cistus salvifolius	152
Cruciata laevipes	181
Cypripedium calceolus	114/115
Daboecia cantabrica	76
Dactylorhiza elata	61
Dactylorhiza fuchsii	62
Dactylorhiza insularis	109
Dactylorhiza sambucina	63
Daphne cneorum	84/85
Dryas octopetala	169
Echinospartum horridum	133
Echium vulgare	22
Epipactis helleborine	184
Epipactis microphylla	184
Erica arborea	153
Erica australis	77
Erinus alpinus	87
Eryngium bourgatii	23
Erysimum duriaei	134
Erythronium dens-canis	78
Euphorbia amygdaloides	186
Euphorbia flavicoma	187
Euphrasia alpina	140
Filipendula vulgaris	141
Fritillaria pyrenaica	138/139
Gagea nevadensis	118
Genista hystrix	119
Gentiana alpina	38
Gentiana lutea	116
Gentiana occidentalis	39
Gentiana pyrenaicum	54
Gentiana verna	40
Gentianella campestris	34
Geranium pyrenaicum	43
Geranium sanguineum	64
Geum montanum	120
Globularia nudicaulis	42
Globularia repens	41
Gymnadenia conopsea	65
Helianthemum apenninum	142
Helianthemum nummularium (ssp)	86
Helianthemum nummularium	121
Helleborus viridis	185
Hepatica nobilis	30/31
Hieracium mixtum (ssp)	122
Himantoglossum hircinum	143
Iberis carnosa	170
Iberis sempervirens	171
Iris latifolia	35
Jasione laevis	24
Lilium pyrenaicum	123
Linaria alpina	55
Linaria elegans	55
Linaria supina	135
Linum narbonense	25
Linum viscosum	66
Lithodora diffusa	36
Lithospermum purpurocaerulea	32
Lonicera etrusca	117
Lotus alpinus	108
Lotus corniculatus	108

Mathiola fruticulosa	88
Melittis melissophyllum	79
Muscari comosum	45
Muscari neglectum	46
Narcissus abscissus	124
Narcissus asturiensis	125
Narcissus nobilis leoninus	126
Narcissus triandrus	127
Nigritella nigra	100
Onobrychis argentea	67
Ophrys apifera	68/69
Ophrys fusca	182
Ophrys insectifera	182
Ophrys lutea	183
Ophrys sphegodes	183
Ophrys tenthredinifera	70/71
Orchis coriophora	47
Orchis mascula	48
Orchis morio	49
Orchis papilionacea	72/73
Orchis purpurea	50
Orchis ustulata	51
Orobanche species	137
Papaver cambrica	110
Pedicularis verticillata	89
Petrocallis pyrenaica	90
Petrocoptis pyrenaica	91
Phyteuma charmelii	52
Pinguicula grandiflora	37
Platanthera chlorantha	144
Polygala alpestris	26
Polygala comosa	74
Polygonatum multiflorum	147
Polygonatum odoratum	147
Primula elatior	128
Primula hirsuta	92
Prunus padus	148
Pulsatilla alpina	154
Pulsatilla alpina (ssp)	154
Pulsatilla rubra (ssp)	105
Pulsatilla vernalis	155
Ramonda myconi	80/81
Ranunculus aconitifolius	156
Ranunculus amplexicaulis	157
Ranunculus aquatilis	158
Ranunculus parnassifolius	172/173
Ranunculus pyrenaeus	159
Reseda suffructicosa	145
Rhinanthus sp	111
Saponaria ocymoides	93
Saxifraga aretioides	136
Saxifraga canaliculata	174
Saxifraga conifera	175
Saxifraga longifolia	176/177
Saxifraga pubescens	178
Scilla liliohyacinthus	33
Scilla verna	27
Sedum album	179
Sempervivum arachnoideum	188
Serapias cordigera	101
Serapias lingua	102
Serapias parviflora	103
Silene acaulis	94/95
Teesdaliopsis conferta	160
Teucrium pyrenaicum	161
Thymus capitata	53
Thymus serpyllum	53
Trifolium alpinum	96
Trollius europeaus	112
Vaccinium myrtllus	104
Valeriana montana	82
Veronica ponae	28
Vicia pyrenaica	97
Viola bubanii	29
Viola cornuta	29
Viola pyrenaica	29

Index - English

Aconite-leaved buttercup	156
Alpine avens	12
Alpine clover	96
Alpine eyebright	140
Alpine milkwort	26
Alpine mouse-ear	168
Alpine pasque flower	154
Alpine toadflax	55
Angel's tears daffodil	127
Asturian daffodil	125
Barton's orchid	109
Bastard balm	79
Beautiful flax	25
Bee orchid	68/69
Bilberry	104
Bird cherry	148
Bird's foot trefoil	108
Bloody cranesbill	64
Blue gromwell	32
Broad-leaved helleborine	184
Broomrape	137
Bug orchid	47
Bumblebee hawkweed	122
Burnt orchid	51
Cantabrian anemone	150
Carduncellus	21
Clasped-leaf buttercup	157
Cobweb houseleek	188
Common rockrose	121
Common snapdragon	98/99
Common Solomon's seal	147
Common spotted marsh orchid	62
Common water-crowfoot	158
Cone saxifrage	175
Creeping globularia	41
Creeping snapdragon	132
Crosswort	181
Dark pasque flower	105
Dog's tooth violet	78
Dragonmouth	44
Dropwort	141
Dull ophrys	182
Early purple orchid	48
Early spider orchid	183
Echinospartum	133
Elder-flowered orchid	63
English iris	35
Etruscan honeysuckle	117
Evergreen candytuft	171
Fairy foxglove	87
Field gentian	34
Fly orchid	182
Fragrant orchid	65
Garland flower	84/85
Globe flower	112
Grape hyacinth	46
Great yellow gentian	116
Greater butterfly orchid	144
Green hellebore	185
Green-winged orchid	49
Hairy rock jasmine	164/165
Hairy saxifrage	178
Heart flowered orchid	101
Hedgehog gorse	119
Hepatica	30/31
Hirsute primrose	92
Horned pansy	29
Kidney vetch	58
Lady orchid	50
Lady's slipper orchid	114/115
Large-flowered butterwort	37
Leafless-stemmed globularia	42
Leon daffodil	126
Lizard orchid	143
Man orchid	180
Marsh marigold	107
Moss campion	94/95
Mossy saxifrage	174
Mountain avens	169
Mountain sandwort	166
Mountain valerian	82
Narcissus-flowered anemone	149
Narrow-leaved valerian	60
Oxlip	128
Parnassus buttercup	172/173
Petrocoptis	91
Pink butterfly orchid	72/73
Pyramidal orchid	56/57

Pyrenean buttercup	159	Tongue orchid	102
Pyrenean columbine	18	Treacle mustard	134
Pyrenean cranesbill	43	Tree heather	153
Pyrenean fritillary	138/139	Trumpet daffodil	124
Pyrenean gagea	118	Tufted milkwort	74
Pyrenean gentian	54	Vandelli's rock jasmine	162/163
Pyrenean germander	161	Vanilla orchid	100
Pyrenean hyacinth	19	Viper's bugloss	22
Pyrenean pheasant's eye	129	Vitaliana	130/131
Pyrenean rampion	52	Welsh poppy	110
Pyrenean rockrose	86	White asphodel	151
Pyrenean saxifrage	176/177	White rockrose	142
Pyrenean sea-holly	23	White stonecrop	179
Pyrenean squill	33	Whorled lousewort	89
Pyrenean thistle	83	Wild thyme	53
Pyrenean toadflax	135	Winged broom	113
Pyrenean trumpet gentian	39	Wood anemone	146
Pyrenean vetch	97	Wood spurge	186
Pyrenean whitlow-grass	90	Woodruff	167
Radish leaved bittercress	59	Yellow onion	106
Ramonda	80/81	Yellow ophrys	183
Red helleborine	75	Yellow rattle	111
Robust marsh orchid	61	Yellow saxifrage	136
Rock soapwort	93	Yellow spurge	187
Sad stock	88	Yellow Turk's cap lily	123
Sage leaved cistus	152		
Sawfly orchid	70/71		
Scrambling gromwell	36		
Sheep's bit	24		
Silvery sainfoin	67		
Small flowered tongue orchid	103		
Small-leaved helleborine	184		
Southern gentian	38		
Spanish heath	77		
Spiked Pyrenean speedwell	28		
Spoon-leaved candytuft	170		
Spreading bellflower	20		
Spring gentian	40		
Spring pasque flower	155		
Spring squill	27		
St Daboec's heath	76		
Sticky flax	66		
Tall mignonette	145		
Tassel hyacinth	45		
Teesdaliopsis	160		